Quarto is the authority on a wide range of topics.
Quarto educates, entertains, and enriches the lives of our readers—
enthusiasts and lovers of hands-on living.
www.quartoknows.com

© 2017 Quarto Publishing Group USA Inc.
Published by Walter Foster Jr.,
an imprint of The Quarto Group
All rights reserved. Walter Foster Jr. is a registered trademark.

Written by Joe Rhatigan
Illustrated by Celeste Aires

6 Orchard Road, Suite 100
Lake Forest, CA 92630
quartoknows.com
Visit our blogs at quartoknows.com

Printed in China
1 3 5 7 9 10 8 6 4 2

MIX
Paper from
responsible sources
FSC® C104723

50
WACKY
IINVENTIONS
THROUGHOUT HISTORY

Weird inventions that seem
too crazy to be real!

Written by Joe Rhatigan
Illustrated by Celeste Aires

TABLE OF CONTENTS

THE CRAZIEST CONTRAPTIONS

Have you ever wanted to fly away on a giant drone? Take a snake for a walk? Sleep on a cloud?

Are there days when you wish you had air conditioners for your armpits?

Inventors are dreamers who come up with creative solutions to problems or new ways to do things. Some of these inventions are wonderful and life changing. Others are not very helpful at all. And others are really incredibly wacky.

This book is about the wacky ones: the giant drones, the snake leashes, the cloud couches, and the armpit coolers. Many of these inventions exist as actual products people can buy. Some were never built because they were just too weird. But at one point, each of the wild wonders in this book was thought up by someone who wanted to earn some money and perhaps also make the world a better place.

Enjoy this trip through the wacky world of gadgets and contraptions. Maybe one of these will lead you to come up with your own awesome (or weird) invention!

NO. 1
SIMPLY ALARMING

The problem with alarm clocks is that people ignore them and oversleep anyway. Inventors have been trying to solve this problem for years. The time-alarm bed invention solved the problem, but caused a different one. It didn't just set off an alarm when it was time to get up. If you didn't act quickly, the bed also tipped sideways, tossing you onto the floor. Yes, it woke you up, but it could lead to injury (or at least a grumpy start to your day).

DID IT WAKE UP THE WORLD?

The time-alarm bed was invented by George Seaman way back in 1892. It didn't become popular; people decided it was better to be late than be thrown to the floor every morning.

NO. 2
PORTABLE PETS

Cats sit on the kitchen table and prowl the great outdoors, and dogs go for walks with their owners. But small furry critters only get a cage! Inventor Brice Belisle tried to fix that with his line of pet clothing. No, this isn't clothing you put on your pet—it's clothing you wear with spaces to put your pets inside! One item, a vest, includes a series of tubes that wrap around your body. Place your small critters inside, and they get to spend the day with you.

IMAGINE THE POSSIBILITIES!

At this point, pet display clothing is still a dream. But imagine what you could wear: Hamster hats? Fish footwear? Gerbil jeans? Rodent robes? Snake skirts? Turtle T-shirts? Imagine wearing all of these at the same time.

NO. 3
WATCH AND RIDE

You want to watch TV, but your parents want you to go outside and play. With 123GoTV everyone's happy. In order to watch your favorite show, you have to pedal a stationary bike. Stop pedaling and the TV goes blank. It's exercise and entertainment at the same time. And it's fun...as long as you're not watching a three-hour movie.

DID THE WHEELS KEEP TURNING?

No! 123GoTV was sold for a brief time before the company that made it went out of business. But that hasn't stopped other inventors from creating stationary bikes that generate electricity, do the laundry, and pump water from wells.

NO. 4
SOGGY DOGGY

It's a fact of life: dogs get dirty. Also, many dogs absolutely hate taking baths. That's why students in Thailand invented a machine that acts just like a canine car wash. Place your pet in the contraption and press some buttons. Warm, sudsy water sprays the dog clean while brushes move back and forth over and under the dog. A few minutes later, the dog comes out sopping wet—and clean.

GREAT MINDS THINK ALIKE

A French inventor created the Dog-O-Matic, which looks a little too much like a washing machine—thankfully without the spin cycle. This invention also blow dries the dog after the bath.

NO. 5
H2 GO!

It's a car! It's a boat! It drives! It floats! Beginning in 1961, Americans were able to buy the Amphicar Model 770, a car that was also a boat. Was it a very good car? Not really. Was it a reliable boat? No. But that didn't stop nearly 4,000 Amphicars from being built and sold. The Quandt Group in Germany stopped making the vehicle in 1967. People just didn't need a car that swam. That's what bridges are for.

HISTORICALLY HYSTERICAL

President Lyndon Johnson owned an Amphicar. He liked to give people rides and scare them by driving into a lake. The president would yell, "The brakes don't work! We're going in!"

NO. 6
BIRD BRAINED

Don't you hate when nature runs away from you when all you want to do is check it out? In 1998, David M. Leslie invented a device that lets nature—especially the flying kind—come to you. This hat comes with its very own bird feeders. All you have to do is put it on and stand still. Don't move a muscle! And don't scratch your nose...or sneeze.

HUMAN BIRD FEEDER

Warning! Use of this product for long periods of time may lead to birds building nests in your hair. Make sure birds do not confuse your ears for bird feeders. Do not wear nice clothes when using this product, and do not open your mouth.

NO. 7
THE HAT-IO

In the 1940s, radios were as big as TV sets. That didn't stop sixteen-year-old Olin Mumford from inventing one of the first radios you could take with you. He created this radio helmet because he wanted to listen to his favorite shows anywhere. This radio hat included headphones, vacuum tubes, batteries, dials, and a giant antenna.

DID ANYONE TUNE IN?

Olin and his invention got some attention in newspapers. But his radio hat didn't take off because it was too heavy. Once the transistor was invented a few years later, portable radios became all the rage.

NO. 8
THE WEED WACKY

The Wonder Boy X-100 was invented in 1957 by Simplicity Manufacturing. This crazy contraption took a simple problem—cutting the grass—and solved it with a space-age, air-conditioned mower that would look more at home on Mars. This goofy golf cart promised to cut the grass, vacuum the lawn, spray weed killer, and plow snow. Meanwhile, the operator worked from the comfort of a domed control center that even had a telephone.

DID IT MAKE THE CUT?

Some inventions seek to make doing chores easier or more comfortable. Sometimes, like with the X-100, they overdo it. Called the "Lazy Man's Power Mower," this invention was never made. That's probably because it should have been called the Crazy Man's Power Mower.

NO. 9
MANY STRINGS ATTACHED

In the 1980s, jazz guitarist Pat Metheny wanted a new guitar. He asked master luthier (a maker of stringed instruments) Linda Manzer for a guitar with "as many strings as possible." Two years later, Manzer unveiled the Pikasso—named because it looks like something out of one of Pablo Picasso's cubist paintings. A regular guitar has one neck, one sound hole, and six strings. The Pikasso has four necks, two sound holes, and 42 strings.

TELL ME MORE!

Pat Metheny can actually play the Pikasso, and you can hear it on several of his recordings. Manzer estimated it took 1,000 hours to build this crazy guitar.

NO. 10
FOR THE BIRDS

Birds make great pets. But unless you keep them in a cage, they poop on your head and the furniture. And cages aren't much fun! That's why Lorraine Moore invented FlightSuits, which are diapers for birds. These poop catchers come in different sizes and colors. You can also dress up your bird as a pirate, Santa Claus, or an Easter Bunny, complete with bunny ears.

DID THIS IDEA FLY?

As strange as putting a diaper on a bird may seem, FlightSuits have been sold all around the world for nearly twenty years. And the birds don't seem to mind at all.

NO. 11
THE SIBLING SEPARATOR

Do your parents constantly warn you to behave in the back seat of the car? Are they one step from "turning this car around"? If so, you may need this simple yet effective divider. Place it between fighting brothers and sisters, and the rest of the ride will be peaceful. The divider could also have pockets for your stuff.

DID IT DIVIDE AND CONQUER?

There are a few different backseat dividers your parents can buy to keep you and your brothers, sisters, and pets separated. Show them this page, and they will probably order one (or more) right away.

NO. 12
A WHEELIE BAD IDEA

Early car inventions were modeled after horse-drawn carriages, which had four wheels. In the early 1930s, Dr. John Purves wondered whether or not we could simplify things and just drive a wheel. He invented the Dynasphere, a giant, 10-foot-tall, doughnut-shaped wheel car that held a driver and three passengers. Step inside the wheel, start the engine, and hope you don't get a flat!

DID IT TAKE OFF?

While the Dynasphere drove up to 30 miles per hour, it couldn't steer (you had to lean one way or the other), go, or stop very well. And if you were really unlucky, there was a chance the driver and passengers would spin head over heels like a hamster that stops running in its wheel.

NO. 13
NOSE PECKER

There are times when you just don't have a free finger to operate a smartphone or tablet. That's why there's Finger-Nose. Strap it on, place it over your nose, and peck away. Sure, you look like Pinocchio, but now you can leave your hands free to play in the mud, knead some dough, or knit a scarf. The only thing you can't do is scratch your nose.

MEET THE INVENTOR

Dominic Wilcox invented the Finger-Nose because he likes to use his smartphone while taking a bath. He also invented stickers designed to make your beautiful bike or car look rusted and scratched so no one will want to steal it.

NO. 14
HEAD IN THE CLOUDS

The Chinese design firm D.K. & Wei was on cloud nine when their Cloud Sofa won Honorable Mention at the 2009 RELAX Furniture Concept Contest. Their idea was to create a couch or chair that not only looks and feels like a super comfy cloud, but also floats! Magnets in the base and in the cloud create a force that keeps the cloud from crashing to the floor. So far, this is still only an idea, so you can't sleep in the clouds quite yet.

GREAT MINDS THINK ALIKE

In 1989, inventor William Calderwood patented his idea for Lighter-Than-Air Furniture. He imagined beds, chairs, and sofas that could be filled with helium so they would float to the ceiling when you weren't using them. This would free up floor space in tiny rooms or apartments.

NO. 15
THIS MOVIE STINKS!

In 1960, moviegoers were promised not just sights and sounds, but also smells. The Cinestage Theatre in Chicago used an invention called Smell-O-Vision. It released perfumes and other odors during certain parts of movies. Large fans blew the smells through pipes that led to vents underneath the audience members' seats. Too bad Smell-O-Vision made too much noise and most people didn't smell anything until after the scene was over.

WILL MOVIES MAKE SCENTS?

Director John Waters released an "odorama" version of one of his movies. Every audience member received a scratch-and-sniff card. When a number flashed on the screen, you scratched off that number on the card and sniffed. This simpler invention has been used a few times since, but it hasn't taken off either.

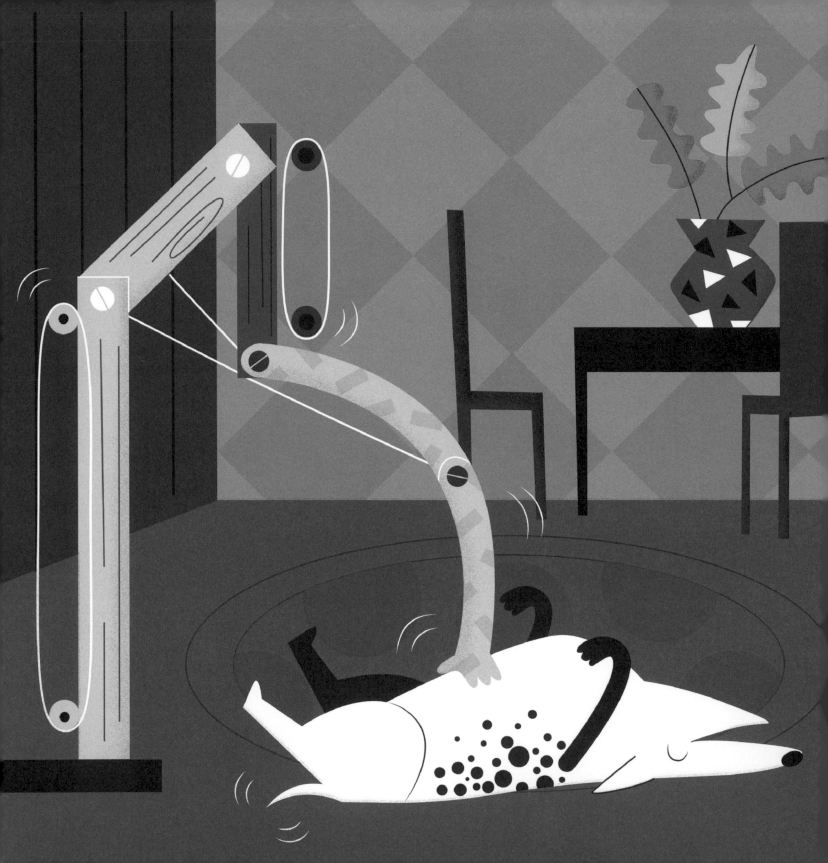

NO. 16
HEAD SCRATCHER

Do you worry about your dog while you're at school? In 1989, inventor Rita Della Vecchia created the Pet Petter—a mechanical arm and hand that does the petting while you're away. Your dog walks to the device and waits for it to turn on. In a moment, your pet is being petted and scratched as if you were there. Maybe now your pooch will stop eating your shoes!

TELL ME MORE!

According to the patent application, the arm would be fully adjustable to handle any size dog. Simply raise or lower the arm to custom fit your pet. The petter would also include an "electronic eye" that senses when your dog is in the right position and ready for some love. Sadly, this invention is still in the planning stages.

NO. 17
FULLY ARMED

If two hands are better than one, imagine how much better life would be with four (or more) hands! Researchers at the Massachusetts Institute of Technology (MIT) have created robotic arms you wear on your back. The arms can reach over your shoulders or out on either side. They can help with lifting heavy things, opening doors when your hands are full, or scratching your head while you're playing the drums.

MEET THE INVENTORS

Since it was founded in 1861, MIT students and teachers have come up with tons of awesome inventions in the worlds of technology, science, healthcare, and more. Just a few MIT inventions include the transistor radio, the minicomputer, the GPS, the microchip, and Clocky (see page 101)!

NO. 18
PIT PURIFIERS

Hot and sweaty in a stifling classroom? Now you can raise your hand without worrying about pit stains or stinky odors. Why? Because you're using Thanko's armpit air conditioners. These tiny fans clip onto your sleeves and direct a refreshing breeze right onto those pee-yew pits. High-five anyone at any time! Raise both hands! Hang from the monkey bars! Put your hands in the air like you just don't care!

TELL ME MORE!

Small, light, and barely noticeable, the armpit air conditioner can be clipped near any body part that is just too hot. (For instance, clip it to your collar if your back is sweaty.) It will keep you breezy for up to nine hours, and if your batteries die, you can connect it to a battery pack or a smart phone.

FULL OF HOT AIR

Wouldn't you love having a robot that cleaned your room and took you places? Robots may seem like modern inventions, but people have been creating different kinds for more than 150 years. One of the first was the Steam Man. It was invented and built in the 1860s, before electricity. It had a small engine and boiler in its chest that moved the robot's legs so it could pull a carriage. Steam came out of the robot's top hat.

HISTORICALLY HYSTERICAL

The Steam Man could supposedly travel a mile a minute. However, it had trouble on rough dirt trails or other uneven surfaces. Some reporters at the time questioned whether it even worked at all. It probably didn't! But its invention did lead to some of the first science fiction stories about robots. And it started the robot craze that continues to this day.

NO. 20
WHAT'S UP?

Inventor John Holding was tired of not being able to read his newspaper on crowded trains. He solved this problem by inventing a pair of reading glasses that let him read his newspaper or a book above his head. The glasses use mirrors to reflect the pages right into your eyes.

DID ANYONE SEE THE LIGHT?

While the invention didn't really catch on, folks found another use for these glasses. By reversing the mirrors, you can read in bed without sitting up. These "prism glasses" have been around for a long time and are still available for purchase.

NO. 21
POWER BALL

One out of five people in the world don't have electricity. The company Uncharted Play thinks it has a solution: the Soccket, a soccer ball that stores energy every time it's rolled or kicked. Playing with the Soccket for one hour provides three hours of lamplight. So now kids with little access to electricity can play all day and do their homework at night. The ball can also be used to charge cellphones and, one day, may power water purifiers, hotplates, and mini-refrigerators.

WILL IT SCORE?

Uncharted Play hopes to deliver more than 1 million Soccket balls to children in poor countries by the year 2020. They have also developed a jump rope that stores energy every time you jump.

NO. 22
BABY BOOSTER

Soon after the invention of the automobile, people started thinking of more things they could attach motors to. In 1922, someone thought, "Hey, how about a motorized baby carriage?" This carriage had a fifth wheel with a gasoline-powered motor attached. It promised to go only four miles per hour (6 kph) and to never wake up the baby. The carriage also had a platform for the nanny to stand on.

GREAT MINDS THINK ALIKE
The British company Quinny is developing a stroller with a skateboard attached to the back so parents can take their kids out for a "roll" instead of a "stroll."

NO. 23
A REAL KICK IN THE PANTS

If you're ever angry at yourself for forgetting to do your chores or your homework, get over to eastern North Carolina, where you can give yourself a kick in the rear. How? With Thomas Haywood's self-kicking machine. Haywood had the contraption built and placed in front of his general store. He said he wanted it for people who "get so disgusted they'd like to kick themselves." It's easy to use. Simply bend over, turn the crank, and wait for the shoes on a wheel to kick you—over and over.

HISTORICALLY HYSTERICAL

Built in 1937, the self-kicking machine attracted national attention as movie stars and politicians took turns giving themselves the boot. President Harry S. Truman supposedly inspected the machine, but there is no evidence that he gave himself a kick. A replica of the invention resides in the same place.

NO. 24
ROCK-A-BYE BATHTUB

In the 1890s and early 1900s, people thought moving and splashing water was healthy, so many rocking bathtubs were invented and sold. One problem was that water always ended up on the floor. This invention solved the splashing problem by creating a "drape" that went all the way up to your neck. Rock away!

TELL ME MORE!

Rocking bathtubs were meant to mimic the movement of rivers and oceans. This treatment was supposed to increase blood circulation, calm the nerves, and cure many diseases. Psst...it didn't do any of those things.

NO. 25
OH, BUOY!

Back in the 1870s, the inventor Traugott Beek thought of a great way to keep people afloat and alive in case of a shipwreck. His life preserver was a suit made of waterproof canvas and metal rings. You raised it over your body, closed the hood, and floated away. Inside, you could enjoy food, water, and a little bit of wiggle room as you waited to be rescued. Meanwhile, the metal rings protected you from sharp rocks and sharks.

DID THIS IDEA FLOAT?

There is no evidence that this lifesaving device was ever actually built. Why not? Well, for one thing, how did it float? A person's body weight, along with the metal rings, would most likely sink this strange-looking costume.

NO. 26
DIRTY DIAPER DETECTOR

Babies pee. Babies poop. Diapers get saggy and leaky. And sometimes parents or babysitters forget to change them. Now, thanks to modern technology, they can place a warning device inside the diaper. This wireless detector flashes a red light and plays a pleasant melody when it senses poo or pee. Of course, now parents have to remove the soaking wet and poopy detector when they finally get around to changing the diaper. Yuck!

DID IT WIPE UP?

There are a few different diaper detectors available for sale. However, most people still rely on nature's very own diaper alarm system: the crying baby.

NO. 27
T.P. TOP HAT

"Chindogu" is the Japanese art of inventing silly and useless gadgets to solve problems. The best example of chindogu is the Toilet Paper Hat. It makes sure you always have a tissue handy, which is helpful when you have a cold. But you will also look very silly with a roll of toilet paper stuck on your head.

TELL ME MORE!

Here are a few more useless and silly chindogu inventions: A tie that is also a small umbrella, a fork with an attached fan to cool down hot food, and a plastic case for a banana.

NO. 28
THE INJURY STICK

A 1960 television ad for the Hop Rod called this toy "the world's first powerized pogo stick," as if that was a good thing. Instead of letting your own weight push down on a spring that sent you back up in the air, the Hop Rod used a gasoline engine. People who actually tried it reported being able to see into second-story windows as they jumped. They also reported multiple injuries.

DANGER ZONE

Warning! This pogo stick has a gas-powered motor. If you jump down hard on the pogo stick, it will send you skyward. If you land at an angle, you will be sent sideways to certain injury. The Hop Rod is no longer for sale. Why? It was crazy dangerous.

NO. 29
GRASSY AND CLASSY

Now you can get closer to nature with Terra! It's lawn furniture that is made out of actual lawn. Order the kit online, build the cardboard frame, fill it with clay and dirt, plant grass seeds, and wait. In about two months you will have a grass chair, couch, or love seat. It's the only furniture you will ever have to mow.

GREAT MINDS THINK ALIKE

You can also grow indoor plant furniture. One item, called the Vege-Table, is an indoor garden that also acts as a coffee table. Another is a bath mat made out of moss. It feels good on your feet after a hot shower, and the moss loves the moist bathroom environment.

NO. 30
LIKE TO FLIKE

If you have ever seen a drone and thought, "wouldn't it be great if there was a drone big enough to fly," then you're not alone. A group of engineers in Hungary have created the Flike, the world's first manned "tricopter." Although the Flike is still being tested, it recently had its first successful test run. When completed, it will be able to stay in the air for up to one hour and travel more than 60 miles an hour (100 kph).

GREAT MINDS THINK ALIKE

Two London inventors have created the Paravelo, a bicycle that can take you 4,000 feet (1,200 meters) up into the air. The bike comes with a large propeller that fills a fabric wing (or parasail) with air, lifting the bike off the ground. You can spend three hours in the air and travel up to 25 miles per hour (40 kph).

NO. 31
BOUNCY SEAT

In our world of exercise bikes and treadmills, it's hard to believe there was a stationary horse exercise machine available more than 120 years ago. According to ads, the Hercules Horse-Action Saddle was "a perfect substitute for the live horse." The machine had a series of springs and three settings: gallop, canter, and trot. You bounced up and down to get it going.

TELL ME MORE!

Ads for this machine promised to promote good spirits, quicken the circulation, stimulate the liver, reduce corpulence, create appetite, and cure indigestion and gout. One ad even said that the Princess of Wales ordered one!

NO. 32
BOING-BOING BOOTS

Imagine being able to jump like a kangaroo on your way to school! The Pyon Pyon jumping shoes have springs on the bottom that provide serious leaping power with every step. The harder you step or jump, the higher you leap. The term "pyon pyon" is Japanese for "boing boing" or "bounce bounce."

MEET THE INVENTOR

Dr. Yoshiro Nakamatsu is a Japanese inventor who claims to have created more than 4,000 inventions. He gets his ideas from holding his breath underwater for as long as possible. He invented a waterproof notebook and pencil to help him write down his ideas.

NO. 33
TRIKE 'N' MOW

Most people want to keep their children away from sharp blades. But the inventor of this lawn mower tricycle would rather the kids help out in the garden. This three-wheeled toy/grass cutter was invented as a quiet and gas-free solution to loud and smelly gas mowers. Also, parents could enjoy their quiet home while their loud and smelly kids worked away outside.

DID IT MOW DOWN THE COMPETITION?

Although finding a greener way to cut the grass while getting some good exercise is a wonderful idea, nobody wanted their kids to lose their fingers and toes for a well-kept lawn.

NO. 34
PUPPY PROTECTOR

The next time it's raining cats and dogs, keep your canine dry with this unique umbrella. Attached to a harness around the pup's middle, the umbrella opens up to completely cover and protect your dog while she goes about her business.

GREAT MINDS THINK ALIKE

There are a few different doggy umbrellas you can buy...just not this one. And if you want to keep your puppy's paws dry too, you can choose from several different types of rain boots.

NO. 35
CATCHER'S CAGE

Catching a fastball can hurt—even when you're wearing a glove. And the gloves used in the early 1900s didn't provide much protection. While baseball players and inventors worked on creating bigger and better gloves, inventor James Bennett tried something different. He came up with a catcher's cage. With this loony device, catchers simply let a pitched ball hit them in the chest, where the wire cage "caught" it and then released it through a hole in the bottom.

DID IT CATCH ON?

Bennett tried for years to get players and investors interested in his cage, as well as his idea for a two-handed catcher's glove. But gloves, known as *mitts*, were simply much easier and more comfortable to use.

NO. 36
FOWL-FOCALS

Chickens don't need help reading the newspaper. Why? Because they can't read! However, in 1903, Andrew Jackson Jr. patented chicken eyeglasses anyway. Why? He believed the glasses would keep the birds from pecking each other's eyes out! Yes, this is a real problem with birds in captivity. And for nearly seventy years, many farmers bought tiny eyeglasses for their chickens.

TELL ME MORE!

Some thought rose-tinted glasses worked even better, and these were quite popular for several years. Thousands of eye protectors were sold, and farmers said the chickens stopped pecking on each other. Recently, a few companies have started making eyeglasses for chickens again.

NO. 37
SOMETHING FISHY

This 1920 invention is a wearable submarine. The giant fish head goes over your own head, leaving your arms free and your legs in two rubber tubes. Inside there's a motor and an air storage tank. Simply put the suit on, turn on the engine, and... most likely sink to the bottom of the ocean.

GREAT MINDS THINK ALIKE

Seabreacher is a company that manufactures diving machines in the shape of whales, sharks, and fish. These powerboats look like jet-fighter sea creatures and can race across the water, dive, and then jump out again, like a dolphin or whale.

NO. 38
BALLOON-ATICS

Balloons bring festive cheer to birthdays, anniversaries, and other celebrations. And with this invention, they can also keep you from getting a sunburn. Just fill this balloon-like sun shade with helium, attach it to yourself with the shoulder straps, and be on your merry way. This handy contraption could also be used to protect against rain.

DID ITS BUBBLE BURST?

Even though it might be nice to forget about applying sunscreen, the balloon would really only protect you when the sun is directly overhead. And while it would also be nice to have both hands free, any sort of wind would blow you away.

NO. 39
THE BODY BIKE

Imagine a bicycle with no pedals, gears, a seat, or even a frame. In 2004, Justin Trenary invented a wheeled device that turned a human into a bike (and could easily transform a healthy person into a very injured one). Strap the back wheel to your legs, hold onto the front wheel with both hands, find a big hill, and ask someone for a push.

DID IT OUTRACE THE COMPETITION?

This bike was designed for downhill racing—and for people who needed more excitement and injuries in their lives. And even though it did include brakes that worked when you squeezed your knees, this body bike was never built.

NO. 40
SLITHER YOUR SNAKE

Dogs and cats get to enjoy the great outdoors. If you take a snake outside, however, it is likely to slither away and scare the neighbors. This snake collar and tether was invented so your pet reptile could enjoy sunlight, grass, and any small critters it comes across—without running away from home.

DID IT SHIMMY?

If this invention had been a success, we would "slither" our snakes, much the way we "walk" our dogs. So even though other reptiles such as lizards (and even turtles) have harnesses and leashes, snakes are still waiting for a better tether.

NO. 41
GIMME FIVE

Sports fans surrounded by their friends have many ways to celebrate their team's touchdown, home run, clutch basket, or goal. One of the best is the *high five*, in which hands are raised and slapped together. Sports fans sitting alone in their living rooms still need to celebrate. Now they can use this wall-mounted arm and hand. Give it a slap and listen as the hand plays the pre-recorded roar of a crowd.

DID IT SCORE?
The high-five arm was never built by its inventor. So if you're watching a game by yourself, you still have to high-five yourself. Hey, wait...isn't that clapping?

NO. 42
SNOT A BAD IDEA

Why do so many people love to wipe their noses on their sleeves? Really...why? Well, this invention allows you to wipe away—right onto a conveniently placed tissue box on the wrist. You can either pull a tissue out and use it, or just bring the device up to your nose and wipe. What could be easier?!

GREAT MINDS THINK ALIKE

In 1928, Laura Schneider invented a bracelet that looked pretty but also held lipstick, powder, and a miniature mirror. In 1948, Clifford Robinson invented a wallet that attaches to your wrist. And in 2006, Stacy Cassel invented wrist-worn baby wipes.

NO. 43
WALKIN' & ROLLIN'

There was a lot going on with this nifty 1930s invention. It was a wagon, a treadmill, and a toy—all in one! With the floorboards attached, it was a regular wagon to put stuff in and pull around. Underneath the boards was a set of rollers. Walking on the rollers made the wagon move forward. Turn the wagon upside down and it was a regular treadmill so you could walk in place. Now that's a walkin' wagon.

DID IT ROLL IN THE DOUGH?

Invented as a toy and an exercise machine, it didn't really work as either. First, kids who walked on it moved slower than if they were simply using their feet. Second, slipping on the rollers must have caused injuries. Third...what happens when you're going downhill?

NO. 44
POWERED BY PAWS

Z. Wigg was an 80-year-old retired railroad worker when he decided to invent a new way to both get around town and walk his dog. He created a vehicle with a giant hamster wheel in the center for the dog to walk in. When the dog walked or ran, the giant wheel turned, which engaged a belt-and-pulley system that moved the back wheels. This unique dog walker also had a steering wheel and headlights.

WAS IT TOP DOG?

No dog is going to be happy about being trapped inside a big wheel. And the power a walking dog creates isn't enough to move this crazy contraption quickly or far. Plus, what if you have a Chihuahua?

NO. 45
WALK THIS WAY

Parents are so proud when their babies take their first steps. And while there are lots of fun devices to help kids learn to walk, this 1939 invention takes away all the fun. To teach his young son to walk, a Swiss engineer took two pairs of wooden poles and strapped them to both his legs and the baby's. Every step he took pushed the baby's legs forward. A harness and wire kept the baby from falling over.

WAS IT A RUNAWAY SUCCESS?

Pretty much every kid throughout history has learned to walk without any fancy equipment. They certainly don't need to be strapped to poles and pushed forward like a human puppet!

NO. 46
CRAWL AND CLEAN

This invention started off as a joke. A fake ad in Japan offered the Baby Mop to "make your children work for their keep." It showed a photograph of a cute baby wearing a one-piece outfit with a mop attached. As the baby crawls, the floor gets cleaned. Since the ad went viral, at least two companies now make a real baby mop onesie.

DID IT CLEAN UP?

Even though it is a real invention that solves a real problem (dirty floors), nobody really expects their babies to crawl and clean. But it would still make a great gift for new moms and dads who may not realize what their newborn could do for them.

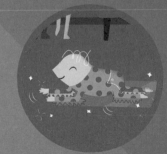

NO. 47
HOT WHEELS

Imagine you and your family are on a long car ride. It's getting late and everyone's hungry. No need to pull over at a fast-food restaurant! Instead, you could eat a piping hot lasagna that was cooked by your car. This 1921 invention sent hot exhaust fumes through a coil that would heat food underneath the front seat. The inventor swore that none of the poisonous gases would get in the food.

GREAT MINDS THINK ALIKE
A popular pizza delivery company now has cars with ovens inside so that your pizza arrives hot and crispy instead of cold and soggy.

NO. 48
CAT LICKER

According to the makers of this device, cats view their humans as large cats. So it probably confuses your cat when they lick you but you never lick them back. Solve that problem now with the Licki Brush. This device is a rubber brush in the shape of a tongue. Clamp it between your teeth and lick your way to a better friendship with your kitty.

WILL IT LICK THE COMPETITION?
The Licki Brush has appeared on several TV shows and in many newspapers and magazines. So, who knows? In a few years, it may seem strange to NOT lick your cat.

NO. 49
A MORNING CHASE

There's nothing quite as refreshing as a quick run early in the morning. And with the Clocky alarm clock, you will certainly be running. You can hit the snooze button once. The second time, the clock takes off on its two wheels. It changes speed and direction and can move around obstacles. If you don't chase and catch Clocky, its alarm will soon go off again. And you will have no idea where it is.

WAS ITS SUCCESS ALARMING?

Its inventor, Gauri Nanda, created Clocky while at MIT (see page 37) because she always overslept for class. In 2005, it won an Ig Nobel Prize, which is given out for a strange or silly scientific achievement. Today it's a bestseller.

NO. 50
WITTY SLICKER

It's really nice when someone shares an umbrella with you during a sudden rainstorm. Inventor Howard Ross found a way to be even nicer: share your raincoat. From the outside, the Double Coat looks like a normal raincoat. But unsnap the insides and it unfolds into a coat for two. Perfect for watching a football game in the rain. But not so good for clapping. Or using a revolving door. Or much of anything else, really.

IMAGINE THE POSSIBILITIES!
There are so many inventions to keep you dry: A double umbrella for keeping two people dry; an umbrella hat that sits right on your head—no hands needed; and an umbrella that acts as a projector for weather maps and movies. Do you have any brainy, rainy invention ideas?

Also in this series

50 Wacky Things Animals Do

describes 50 peculiar animal behaviors that seem too crazy to be true—but are!

50 Wacky Things Humans Do

describes 50 weird, wild, and unbelievable things the body does.